Python (50) Fifty

50 Programming Exercises for Pytho

Book 1

Table of contents

Disclaimer

All content in this book, including text, graphics, and layout, is protected by copyright and intellectual property laws. Unauthorized reproduction, whether in whole or in part, in any format or medium, is strictly prohibited without the prior written consent of the author.

While every effort has been made to ensure the accuracy and reliability of the information provided, the author makes no guarantees and assumes no liability for any errors, omissions, or damages arising from the use of this book's content.

By using this book, the reader acknowledges and accepts all risks associated with the use of the information provided.

Python Interpreter

You can download the latest release of Python from the following link:
www.python.org/downloads/

Alternatively, there are several free online compilers available. A quick web search will quickly lead you to these resources.

The exercises

This book contains 50 exercises, each with solutions, designed for Python beginners (Entry-Level). A detailed overview of the topics covered can be found in any introductory Python programming textbook or through a quick online search.

The exercises are presented in random order, with varying levels of difficulty. This is intentional, as the goal is to offer a tool for assessing your actual knowledge rather than just reviewing specific topics. As you progress, you'll be prompted to recall what you've learned so far, connecting it to the topics listed. You may need to search for a function, method, keyword, or operator you know exists but can't quite remember how to write correctly. This process will help reinforce your understanding and solidify your skills.

Gradually, as you move from one topic to another, you'll develop a broader understanding of Python as a programming language. The individual elements you've studied will begin to come together into more complex sequences of instructions, all aimed at solving specific problems.

How to use this book

There are mainly two perks to reading a book; the first is that it's an incredibly effective, yet underrated, way to expand your mind. The second is that reading allows you to turn those moments in life when you're stuck somewhere, due to circumstances beyond your control, into productive ones. We could also mention that reading provides a great excuse to avoid your boring seatmate from bothering you with trivial chit-chat, but that's another story...

Now, if you're reading these lines, we can assume you're studying Python and therefore need some practice. So, here's the idea. If you have a laptop/tablet etc. handy, then you can skip to the next chapter. But if you don't, here's a simple idea: you can just go back to the ever useful pencil and eraser. Under each exercise, there's some blank space, it wasn't put there by accident, but rather so YOU can use it to write code by hand. It might sound strange, but writing code, rather than typing it, often allows you to memorize the basic syntax more effectively and quickly, and also the indentation (often a source of errors for beginners, no use denying it, we've all been there). Not to mention that keeping your handwriting skills sharp, nowadays, is almost a rarity. And anyway, since you're stuck on a train/bus/whatever without a laptop, where else are you going to type the code? By the way, in the second half of the book, chapter "Solutions 1-50" you'll find the solutions to check if what you've written is correct.

Tips for effective learning

Create a table with 50 empty cells, each representing an exercise to be checked off as it's completed correctly. If, upon finishing the last exercise, there are still empty spaces, restart from exercise #1. Once all cells are filled, move on to new material.

For now, it's not crucial to remember the exact names of functions, methods, keywords, or parameters, as long as you understand how to structure the code to arrive at the correct solution. Memorizing all the elements of Python takes time and plenty of practice. Plus, resources like books or the internet are always available. However, if you haven't checked all the boxes by the end of your first pass, it's recommended to revisit all the exercises, including those you've already solved correctly.

Happy coding!

My Notes

I have intentionally left this page blank for your notes. Feel free to jot down your thoughts, insights, or anything you find useful while working through the exercises.

Exercises 1-50

Exercise 1

Write a Python program that assign the phrase `"Hello World!"` to a variable named `hello`. Use the `print()` function to display the value of the `hello` variable on the screen.

Exercise 2

Write a Python program that does the following:

1. Counts how many times each character appears in the `string = "abcdef abcde abcd abc`
   `ab a"` (including spaces).
2. Displays the count of each character in the format: "The character 'x' appears y times."

Hint: You can use a dictionary to track the count of each character and iterate through the string to update the counts.

Exercise 3

Assign two values of your choice to variables named `base` and `exponent`.
Write a Python program that does the following:
1. Uses the power operator (**) to calculate the result of raising `base` to the power of `exponent`.
2. Prints the result in the format: "base raised to the power of exponent is result."

Exercise 4

Create two variables, A and B, with values of your choice. Write a Python program that does the following:

1. Prints the values of A and B before the swap.
2. Uses a third variable to swap the values of A and B.
3. Prints the values of A and B after the swap.

Exercise 5

Write a Python program that adds the key-value pair 1: "a" to the empty dictionary named d1. Print the updated dictionary.

Exercise 6

The Gauss formula for the sum of the first n natural numbers states that the sum of the numbers from 1 to n is equal to the half-product of n and n+1. The formula is:

$S = n * (n + 1) / 2$

Write a Python program that does the following:

1. Takes a number n as input.
2. Uses the formula to calculate the sum of all natural numbers up to n.
3. Prints the result in the format: "The sum of the first n natural numbers is S."

Exercise 7

Write a Python program that calculates the following sums from the `list = [-1, 3, 6, -4, 5, 8, -7, 1, 4]`:

1. The sum of all negative numbers.
2. The sum of all positive numbers.
3. The sum of all even numbers.
4. The sum of all odd numbers.

Print the sums for each category in a clear format.

Hint: Be sure to properly consider that a number can be both positive and even, or negative and even, or any other combination. Make sure each condition is checked independently.

Exercise 8

Write a Python program that prints all characters from the `string = "Today I am learning to write lines of code with Python"` that have an odd index.

Exercise 9

Write a Python program that:

Asks the user to input the following:

1   An integer.

2   A decimal number.

3   A string.

Prints all the values entered in a clear format.

Exercise 10

Write a Python program that prints all the values in the `dictionary = {1: 'a', 2: 'b'}`.

Exercise 11

Write a Python program that print the following message, dynamically replacing parts of the text with the values of variables:

"The best score of the day is 45%. Your best score reached 35%. You had no chance of winning."

The program should use these variables:
```
1   score = 'best score'
2   a = 0.45 (representing 45%)
3   b = 0.35 (representing 35%)
```
Use the .format () method to insert these variables into the text.

Exercise 12

Write a Python program that does the following:
1. Asks the user to input a single character.
2. Prints the corresponding ASCII value of the entered character using the `ord()` function.
3. Displays the output in the format:
"The character 'x' has an ASCII value of y."

Exercise 13

Write a Python program that does the following:
1. Asks the user to input a number n, representing the size of a list.
2. Prompts the user to enter n numbers to populate the list.
3. Creates two separate sub-lists:
   - One containing all the even numbers.
   - One containing all the odd numbers.
4. Prints both sub-lists.
5. Prints the largest value in each sub-list. If a sub-list is empty, indicate that it contains no numbers.

Exercise 14

Write a Python program that prints every odd number from 1 up to and including 10.

Exercise:

```python
# Print all odd numbers from 1 to 10
for i in range(1, 11, 2):  # Start at 1, increment by 2
    print(i)
```

Exercise 15

Write a Python program that Identifies and prints the words that contain both letters and numbers in the
`string = '1The2 beach 3was45 crowded'`.

Write a Python program that:
1. Asks the user to input a string.
2. Concatenates the first character, the middle character, and the last character of the string.
   - If the string has an even length, the middle character is the one at the lower middle index.
3. Prints the resulting concatenated string.

Exercise 17

Write a Python program that:
1. Defines the following two lists:
   - `function = ['model', 'variant']`
   - `value = [1, 2]`
2. Combines the elements of these lists to create a new list, `result`, where each item from function is paired with each item from value in the format 'function: value'.
3. Prints the resulting list `result`.

Exercise 18

Write a Python program that:

1. Asks the user to input an income value (`income`).
2. Calculates the tax based on the following tax brackets:
   - Up to 10,000: No tax (0%).
   - From 10,001 to 20,000: Taxed at 10%.
   - Over 20,000: Taxed at 20%, with the first 10,000 taxed at 0% and the next 10,000 taxed at 10%.
3. Prints the calculated tax based on the input income.

Exercise 19

Write a Python program that:
1. Asks the user to input two integers.
2. Calculates the product of the two integers.
   - If the product is less than 10, prints the product.
   - If the product is greater than or equal to 10, prints the sum of the two integers.

Exercise 20

Write a Python program that merges `list_1 = [5, 3, 1, 2, 4]` and `list_2 = [7, 9, 8, 10, 6]` into a single list. Then:

1. Sorts the merged list in ascending order.
2. Prints the sorted list.

Exercise 21

Write a Python program that swaps the first element with the last element in the `list = [6, 2, 3, 4, 5, 1]`. Prints the updated list.

Exercise 22

Write a Python program that removes all numeric characters from the `string = '1the 2beach 3was 4crowded5'`. Prints the updated string without numbers.

Exercise 23

Write a Python program that defines the two lists: a = ['c', 'd'] and b = [3, 4]. Then:

1. Combines the corresponding elements from the two lists to create a new list, result, where each element from a is concatenated with the corresponding element from b.
2. Uses the zip() function and avoids nested loops.
3. Prints the resulting list.

Exercise 24

Write a Python program that prints the following pattern:

```
*****
*****
*****
*****
*****
```

Exercise 25

Write a Python program that defines two dictionaries: d1 = {1: 'a', 3: 'c', 4: 'b'} and d2 = {2: 'e', 5: 'd'}. Then:

1. Concatenates the two dictionaries into one.
2. Prints the resulting dictionary.

Exercise 26

Write a Python program that creates a dictionary where:
1. The keys are integers from 1 to n.
2. The values are the squares of the keys.
Prints the resulting dictionary.

Exercise 27

Write a Python program that:
1. Prints the multiplication table for numbers from 1 to 10.
2. Formats the output so that each value is separated by a tab (\t) for better readability.

Output example:

1	2	3	4
2	4	6	8
3	6	9	12
4	8	12	16

Exercise 28

Write a Python program that reverses the digits of a given `number = 1234`. Prints the reversed number.

Exercise 29

Write a Python program that:
1. Asks the user to input a number n.
2. Prints all even numbers starting from 0 up to (but not including) n.
3. Displays the numbers on the same line, separated by spaces.

Exercise 30

Write a Python program that:

1. Asks the user to input two integers using a single `input ()` function, separated by a space.
2. Calculates and prints the sum of the two integers in the format:
   "Sum of a and b = result"

Exercise 31

Write a Python program that:
1. Asks the user to input a year.
2. Checks whether the entered year is a leap year based on the following rules:
    - A year is a leap year if it is divisible by 4 but not divisible by 100.
    - A year is also a leap year if it is divisible by 400.
3. Prints whether the year is a leap year or not in a clear message.

Exercise 32

Write a Python program that:

1. Uses the datetime module to retrieve today's date.
2. Prints today's date in the format day/month/year (e.g., 06/12/2024).

Exercise 33

Write a Python program that rounds the `value = 123.012345` to two decimal places and prints the result.

Exercise 34

Write a Python program that:

1. Asks the user to input the base and height of a right triangle.
2. Checks if either the base or the height is less than or equal to zero. If so, prints an error message indicating that the base and height must be positive numbers.
3. If the values are valid, calculates the area of the triangle using the formula:
   - Area = (base * height) / 2
4. Prints the calculated area.

Exercise 35

Write a Python program that:
1. Asks the user to input an integer.
2. Determines if the number is even or odd using the modulus operator %.
3. Prints a message stating whether the number is even or odd.

Exercise 36

Write a Python program to find and print the greatest number in the `list = [10, 12, 23, 14, 3, 6]`.

Exercise 37

Write a Python program that prints a list of the first 100 integers (from 1 to 100).

Exercise 38

Write a Python program that creates a list of tuples, where each tuple contains a key-value pair, like `t =` `[('a', 1), ('b', 2), ('c', 3)]`.
Then, convert this list of tuples into a dictionary and print the resulting dictionary.

Exercise 39

Write a Python program to create a dictionary that stores the frequency of each character in the `string` = `'consideration'`. Print the resulting dictionary.

Exercise 40

Write a Python program that:
1. Prompts the user to input a number.
2. Checks if the number is divisible by 3, 5, or 7.
3. Prints the results in a single `print()` statement, using string formatting to clearly indicate whether the number is divisible by each of these numbers.

Exercise 41

Write a Python program that removes all empty strings (`' '`) and `None` values from the `list =` `['house', '', 'cat', '', 'chair', None]`. Prints the resulting list.

Exercise 42

Write a Python program that:

1. Prompts the user to input a value from the `list = [1, 2, 3, 1, 2, 4, 3, 1, 5, 4, 6, 4, 3, 2, 1]`.
2. Counts how many times the entered value appears in the list.
3. Prints the result.

Exercise 43

Write a Python program that prints the length of the list = [1, 2, 3, 4, 5, 6] without using the len() function.

Write a Python program that asks the user to input their name and then prints the message:
`"Hello, [username]"`.

Exercise 45

Write a Python program that:
1. Asks the user to enter a string.
2. Prints each character of the string on a separate line.
3. Displays the total number of characters in the string.

Exercise 46

Write a Python program that finds and prints the index positions of every occurrence of the character 'i' in the `string = "I like this song"`.

Exercise 47

Write a Python program that:
1. Defines the `string = "Who could I ever be, then as now, if not myself?"`.
2. Counts the number of vowels in the string, considering both uppercase and lowercase letters.
3. Prints the total number of vowels in the string.

Write a Python program that adds a new key-value pair `6: 'f'` to the `dictionary = {1: 'a', 2: 'b', 3: 'c', 4: 'd', 5: 'e'}`. Print the updated dictionary.

Exercise 49

Write a Python program that:
1. Defines a `dictionary = {'A': 1, 'B': 2, 'C': 3}`.
2. Checks if the key 'A' exists in the dictionary.
3. Prints a message indicating whether the key 'A' is present in the dictionary or not.

Write a Python program that:
1. Defines a `dictionary = {'a': 1, 'b': 2, 'c': 3}`.
    2. Loops through the dictionary and prints each key-value pair in the format: key -> value.

Solution 1

Write a Python program that assign the phrase "Hello World!" to a variable named hello. Use the print() function to display the value of the hello variable on the screen.

Solution:

```
# Step 1: Assign the phrase "Hello World!" to the variable hello
hello = "Hello World!"

# Step 2: Use the print() function to display the value of hello
print(hello)
```

Solution 2

Write a Python program that does the following:
3. Counts how many times each character appears in the `string` = `"abcdef abcde abcd abc` `ab a"` (including spaces).
4. Displays the count of each character in the format: "The character 'x' appears y times."

Hint: You can use a dictionary to track the count of each character and iterate through the string to update the counts.

Solution:

```
# Step 1: Create the string
text = "abcdef abcde abcd abc ab a"

# Step 2: Create an empty dictionary to store character counts
char_count = {}

# Step 3: Count the occurrences of each character in the string
for char in text:
    if char in char_count:
        char_count[char] += 1
    else:
        char_count[char] = 1

# Step 4: Display the count of each character
for char, count in char_count.items():
    print(f"The character '{char}' appears {count} times.")
```

Solution 3

Assign two values of your choice to variables named base and exponent.
Write a Python program that does the following:
3. Uses the power operator (**) to calculate the result of raising base to the power of exponent.
4. Prints the result in the format: "base raised to the power of exponent is result."

Solution:

```python
# Step 1: Assign values to base and exponent
base = 3
exponent = 4

# Step 2: Use the power operator (**) to calculate the result
result = base ** exponent

# Step 3: Print the result in the required format
print(f"{base} raised to the power of {exponent} is {result}.")
```

Solution 4

Create two variables, A and B, with values of your choice. Write a Python program that does the following:
4. Prints the values of A and B before the swap.
5. Uses a third variable to swap the values of A and B.
6. Prints the values of A and B after the swap.

Solution:

```
# Step 1: Assign values to A and B
A = 1
B = 50

# Step 2: Print the initial values of A and B
print(f"Before swap: A = {A}, B = {B}")

# Step 3: Swap the values using a third variable
temp = A
A = B
B = temp

# Step 4: Print the values after the swap
print(f"After swap: A = {A}, B = {B}")
```

Solution 5

Write a Python program that adds the key-value pair 1 : "a" to the empty dictionary named d1. Print the updated dictionary.

Solution:

```
# Step 1: Create an empty dictionary
d1 = {}

# Step 2: Add the key-value pair 1: "a" to the dictionary
d1[1] = 'a'

# Step 3: Print the updated dictionary
print(d1)
```

Solution 6

The Gauss formula for the sum of the first n natural numbers states that the sum of the numbers from 1 to n is equal to the half-product of n and n+1. The formula is:

$S = n * (n + 1) / 2$

Write a Python program that does the following:

4. Takes a number n as input.
5. Uses the formula to calculate the sum of all natural numbers up to n.
6. Prints the result in the format: "The sum of the first n natural numbers is S."

Solution:

```
# Step 1: Take input from the user
n = int(input("Enter a number: "))

# Step 2: Use the Gauss formula to calculate the sum
sum_n = n * (n + 1) // 2  # Use integer division for cleaner output

# Step 3: Print the result
print(f"The sum of the first {n} natural numbers is {sum_n}.")
```

Solution 7

Write a Python program that calculates the following sums from the `list` = `[-1, 3, 6, -4, 5,`
`8, -7, 1, 4]`:
5. The sum of all negative numbers.
6. The sum of all positive numbers.
7. The sum of all even numbers.
8. The sum of all odd numbers.
Print the sums for each category in a clear format.

Hint: Be sure to properly consider that a number can be both positive and even, or negative and even, or any other combination. Make sure each condition is checked independently.

Solution:

```
# Step 1: Define the list
numbers = [-1, 3, 6, -4, 5, 8, -7, 1, 4]

# Step 2: Initialize sums for each category
negative_sum = 0
positive_sum = 0
even_sum = 0
odd_sum = 0

# Step 3: Iterate through the list and calculate sums
for num in numbers:
    if num < 0:
        negative_sum += num
    else:
        positive_sum += num

    if num % 2 == 0:
        even_sum += num
    else:
        odd_sum += num

# Step 4: Print the results
print(f"Sum of negative numbers: {negative_sum}")
print(f"Sum of positive numbers: {positive_sum}")
print(f"Sum of even numbers: {even_sum}")
print(f"Sum of odd numbers: {odd_sum}")
```

Solution 8

Write a Python program that prints all characters from the `string = "Today I am learning to write lines of code with Python"` that have an odd index.

Solution:

```python
# Step 1: Define the string
string = "Today I am learning to write lines of code with Python"

# Step 2: Iterate through characters with odd indices
for i in range(1, len(string), 2):
    print(string[i], end=' ')
```

Solution 9

Write a Python program that:
Asks the user to input the following:
4   An integer.
5   A decimal number.
6   A string.
Prints all the values entered in a clear format.

Solution:

```python
# Step 1: Ask the user for inputs
integer_number = int(input("Enter an integer: "))
decimal_number = float(input("Enter a decimal number: "))
text_string = input("Enter a string: ")

# Step 2: Print the values entered
print(f"Integer entered: {integer_number}")
print(f"Decimal number entered: {decimal_number}")
print(f"String entered: {text_string}")
```

Solution 10

Write a Python program that prints all the values in the `dictionary = {1: 'a', 2: 'b'}`.

Solution:

```python
# Step 1: Create a dictionary with the given key-value pairs
dictionary = {1: 'a', 2: 'b'}

# Step 2: Print each value in the dictionary
for value in dictionary.values():
    print(value)
```

Solution 11

Write a Python program that print the following message, dynamically replacing parts of the text with the values of variables:

"The best score of the day is 45%. Your best score reached 35%. You had no chance of winning."

The program should use these variables:

```
4   score = 'best score'
5   a = 0.45 (representing 45%)
6   b = 0.35 (representing 35%)
```
Use the . format () method to insert these variables into the text.

Solution:

# Step 1: Define the variables
score = "best score"
a = 0.45
b = 0.35

# Step 2: Create the text template with placeholders
text = "The {score} of the day is {a:.0%}. Your {score} reached {b:.0%}. You had no chance of winning."

# Step 3: Format the text with the variables
print(text.format(score=score, a=a, b=b))

Solution 12

Write a Python program that does the following:
4. Asks the user to input a single character.
5. Prints the corresponding ASCII value of the entered character using the ord() function.
6. Displays the output in the format:
"The character 'x' has an ASCII value of y."

Solution:

```
# Step 1: Ask the user to input a character
char = input("Enter a single character: ")

# Step 2: Get the ASCII value of the character
ascii_value = ord(char)

# Step 3: Print the result
print(f"The character '{char}' has an ASCII value of {ascii_value}.")
```

Solution 13

Write a Python program that does the following:
6. Asks the user to input a number n, representing the size of a list.
7. Prompts the user to enter n numbers to populate the list.
8. Creates two separate sub-lists:
   - One containing all the even numbers.
   - One containing all the odd numbers.
9. Prints both sub-lists.
10. Prints the largest value in each sub-list. If a sub-list is empty, indicate that it contains no numbers.

Solution:

```python
# Step 1: Initialize empty lists
numbers = []
even_numbers = []
odd_numbers = []

# Step 2: Get the size of the list
n = int(input("Enter the number of elements in the list: "))

# Step 3: Populate the list with user input
for _ in range(n):
    value = int(input("Enter a number: "))
    numbers.append(value)
    # Step 4: Classify numbers into even or odd
    if value % 2 == 0:
        even_numbers.append(value)
    else:
        odd_numbers.append(value)

# Step 5: Print both sub-lists
print("Even numbers:", even_numbers)
print("Odd numbers:", odd_numbers)

# Step 6: Print the largest value in each sub-list or a message if empty
if even_numbers:
    print("Largest even number:", max(even_numbers))
else:
    print("No even numbers in the list.")

if odd_numbers:
    print("Largest odd number:", max(odd_numbers))
```

```
else:
    print("No odd numbers in the list.")
```

Solution 14

Write a Python program that prints every odd number from 1 up to and including 10.

Solution:

```python
# Print all odd numbers from 1 to 10
for i in range(1, 11, 2):  # Start at 1, increment by 2
    print(i)
```

Solution 15

Write a Python program that Identifies and prints the words that contain both letters and numbers in the `string = '1The2 beach 3was45 crowded'`.

Solution:

```python
# Step 1: Define the string
text = '1The2 beach 3was45 crowded'

# Step 2: Split the string into words
words = text.split()

# Step 3: Check each word
for word in words:
    # Step 4: Check if the word contains both letters and numbers
    has_letters = False
    has_digits = False

    for char in word:
        if char.isalpha():
            has_letters = True
        if char.isdigit():
            has_digits = True

    if has_letters and has_digits:
        print(word)
```

Solution 16

Write a Python program that:
4. Asks the user to input a string.
5. Concatenates the first character, the middle character, and the last character of the string.
   - If the string has an even length, the middle character is the one at the lower middle index.
6. Prints the resulting concatenated string.

Solution:

```python
# Step 1: Ask the user to input a string
string = input("Enter a string: ")

# Step 2: Get the length of the string
length = len(string)

# Step 3: Determine the middle character(s) and concatenate
if length % 2 == 0:  # Even length
    result = string[0] + string[length // 2 - 1] + string[length // 2] + string[-1]
else:  # Odd length
    result = string[0] + string[length // 2] + string[-1]

# Step 4: Print the resulting concatenated string
print("Result:", result)
```

Solution 17

Write a Python program that:

4. Defines the following two lists:
   - `function = ['model', 'variant']`
   - `value = [1, 2]`
5. Combines the elements of these lists to create a new list, `result`, where each item from function is paired with each item from value in the format 'function: value'.
6. Prints the resulting list `result`.

Solution:

```
# Step 1: Define the two lists
function = ['model', 'variant']
value = [1, 2]

# Step 2: Create the result list using a simple loop
result = []

for func in function:
    for val in value:
        result.append(f"{func}: {val}")

# Step 3: Print the resulting list
print(result)
```

Solution 18

Write a Python program that:

4. Asks the user to input an income value (`income`).
5. Calculates the tax based on the following tax brackets:
    - Up to 10,000: No tax (0%).
    - From 10,001 to 20,000: Taxed at 10%.
    - Over 20,000: Taxed at 20%, with the first 10,000 taxed at 0% and the next 10,000 taxed at 10%.
6. Prints the calculated tax based on the input income.

Solution:

```
# Step 1: Ask the user to input their income
income = float(input("Enter your income: "))

# Step 2: Calculate the tax based on the brackets
if income > 20000:
    tax = (income - 20000) * 0.2 + 1000  # 20% on income above 20,000 + 10% on the next 10,000
elif income > 10000:
    tax = (income - 10000) * 0.1  # 10% on income between 10,001 and 20,000
else:
    tax = 0  # No tax for income up to 10,000

# Step 3: Print the calculated tax
print("Tax:", tax)
```

Solution 19

Write a Python program that:

3. Asks the user to input two integers.
4. Calculates the product of the two integers.
   - If the product is less than 10, prints the product.
   - If the product is greater than or equal to 10, prints the sum of the two integers.

Solution:

```python
# Step 1: Ask the user to input two integers
a = int(input("Enter the first integer: "))
b = int(input("Enter the second integer: "))

# Step 2: Calculate the product
product = a * b

# Step 3: Check the conditions and print the appropriate result
if product < 10:
    print("Product =", product)
else:
    print("Sum =", a + b)
```

Write a Python program that merges `list_1 = [5, 3, 1, 2, 4]` and `list_2 = [7, 9, 8, 10, 6]` into a single list. Then:

3. Sorts the merged list in ascending order.
4. Prints the sorted list.

Solution:

```python
# Step 1: Define the two lists
list_1 = [5, 3, 1, 2, 4]
list_2 = [7, 9, 8, 10, 6]

# Step 2: Merge and sort the lists
merged_sorted_list = sorted(list_1 + list_2)

# Step 3: Print the sorted list
print("Sorted list:", merged_sorted_list)
```

Solution 21

Write a Python program that swaps the first element with the last element in the `list = [6, 2, 3, 4, 5, 1]`. Prints the updated list.

Solution:

```
# Step 1: Define the list
my_list = [6, 2, 3, 4, 5, 1]

# Step 2: Swap the first and last elements
my_list[0], my_list[-1] = my_list[-1], my_list[0]

# Step 3: Print the updated list
print("Updated list:", my_list)
```

Solution 22

Write a Python program that removes all numeric characters from the `string = '1the 2beach 3was 4crowded5'`. Prints the updated string without numbers.

Solution:

```python
# Step 1: Define the original string
string = '1the 2beach 3was 4crowded5'

# Step 2: Initialize an empty string to store the updated string
updated_string = ''

# Step 3: Loop through each character in the original string
for char in string:
    # Step 4: Check if the character is not a digit
    if not char.isdigit():
        # Step 5: Add the non-digit character to the updated string
        updated_string += char

# Step 6: Print the updated string
print("Updated string:", updated_string)
```

Solution 23

Write a Python program that defines the two lists: a = `['c', 'd']` and b = `[3, 4]`. Then:

4. Combines the corresponding elements from the two lists to create a new list, `result`, where each element from a is concatenated with the corresponding element from b.
5. Uses the `zip()` function and avoids nested loops.
6. Prints the resulting list.

Solution:

```
# Step 1: Define the two lists
a = ['c', 'd']
b = [3, 4]

# Step 2: Combine corresponding elements using zip() and list comprehension
result = [i + str(j) for i, j in zip(a, b)]

# Step 3: Print the resulting list
print("Resulting list:", result)
```

Solution 24

Write a Python program that prints the following pattern:

```
*****
*****
*****
*****
*****
```

Solution:

```python
# Step 1: Define the number of rows and columns
rows = 5

# Step 2: Use a nested loop to print the pattern
for i in range(rows):  # Outer loop for rows
    for j in range(rows):  # Inner loop for columns
        print('*', end='')  # Print '*' without moving to the next line
    print()  # Move to the next line after each row is printed
```

Solution 25

Write a Python program that defines two dictionaries: d1 = {1: 'a', 3: 'c', 4: 'b'} and d2 = {2: 'e', 5: 'd'}. Then:

3. Concatenates the two dictionaries into one.
4. Prints the resulting dictionary.

Solution:

```python
# Step 1: Define the two dictionaries
d1 = {1: 'a', 3: 'c', 4: 'b'}
d2 = {2: 'e', 5: 'd'}

# Step 2: Create an empty dictionary to store the result
result = {}

# Step 3: Add the key-value pairs from the first dictionary to the result
for key, value in d1.items():
    result[key] = value

# Step 4: Add the key-value pairs from the second dictionary to the result
for key, value in d2.items():
    result[key] = value

# Step 5: Print the resulting dictionary
print("Concatenated dictionary:", result)
```

Solution 26

Write a Python program that creates a dictionary where:
3. The keys are integers from 1 to n.
4. The values are the squares of the keys.
Prints the resulting dictionary.

Solution:

```python
# Step 1: Ask the user for the upper limit
n = int(input("Enter the upper limit (n): "))

# Step 2: Create the dictionary using a dictionary comprehension
squares_dict = {i: i ** 2 for i in range(1, n + 1)}

# Step 3: Print the resulting dictionary
print("Dictionary of squares:", squares_dict)
```

Write a Python program that:

3. Prints the multiplication table for numbers from 1 to 10.
4. Formats the output so that each value is separated by a tab (\t) for better readability.

Output example:

1	2	3	4
2	4	6	8
3	6	9	12
4	8	12	16

Solution:

```python
# Step 1: Loop through the numbers 1 to 10
for i in range(1, 11):
    # Step 2: Loop through the multiplier for the current number
    for j in range(1, 11):
        # Step 3: Print the product, formatted with a tab
        print(i * j, end='\t')
    # Step 4: Move to the next line after completing a row
    print()
```

Solution 28

Write a Python program that reverses the digits of a given `number` = 1234. Prints the reversed number.

Solution:

```python
# Step 1: Define the number to be reversed
num = 1234

# Step 2: Initialize the reversed number
reversed_num = 0

# Step 3: Reverse the digits using a loop
while num != 0:
    digit = num % 10  # Extract the last digit
    reversed_num = reversed_num * 10 + digit  # Append it to the reversed number
    num = num // 10  # Remove the last digit from the original number

# Step 4: Print the reversed number
print("Reversed number:", reversed_num)
```

Solution 29

Write a Python program that:

4. Asks the user to input a number n.
5. Prints all even numbers starting from 0 up to (but not including) n.
6. Displays the numbers on the same line, separated by spaces.

Solution:

```python
# Step 1: Get the input from the user
n = int(input("Enter the upper limit for the series: "))

# Step 2: Loop through numbers from 0 to n, incrementing by 2
for i in range(0, n, 2):
    print(i, end=' ')
```

Solution 30

Write a Python program that:

3. Asks the user to input two integers using a single `input ()` function, separated by a space.
4. Calculates and prints the sum of the two integers in the format:
   "Sum of a and b = result"

Solution:

```python
# Step 1: Prompt the user to enter two integers separated by a space
# Ask the user for two integers
input_string = input("Enter two integers (a and b) separated by a space: ")

# Split the input into two parts
input_list = input_string.split()

# Convert each part into an integer and assign it to variables 'a' and 'b'
a = int(input_list[0])
b = int(input_list[1])

# Step 2: Calculate and print the sum
print("Sum of {} and {} = {}".format(a, b, a + b))
```

Solution 31

Write a Python program that:

4 . Asks the user to input a year.

5 . Checks whether the entered year is a leap year based on the following rules:
- A year is a leap year if it is divisible by 4 but not divisible by 100.
- A year is also a leap year if it is divisible by 400.

6 . Prints whether the year is a leap year or not in a clear message.

Solution:

```python
# Step 1: Prompt the user to enter a year
year = int(input("Enter a year: "))

# Step 2: Check if the year is a leap year
if (year % 4 == 0 and year % 100 != 0) or (year % 400 == 0):
    print(f"{year} is a leap year.")
else:
    print(f"{year} is not a leap year.")
```

Solution 32

Write a Python program that:
3. Uses the datetime module to retrieve today's date.
4. Prints today's date in the format day/month/year (e.g., 06/12/2024).

Solution:

```python
from datetime import datetime

# Get today's date
today = datetime.now()

# Format the date as day/month/year
formatted_date = today.strftime("%d/%m/%Y")

# Print the formatted date
print(formatted_date)
```

Solution 33

Write a Python program that rounds the `value` = `123.012345` to two decimal places and prints the result.

Solution:

```python
# Define the number
number = 123.012345

# Round to two decimal places
rounded_value = round(number, 2)

# Print the result
print("Rounded value:", rounded_value)
```

Solution 34

Write a Python program that:

5. Asks the user to input the base and height of a right triangle.
6. Checks if either the base or the height is less than or equal to zero. If so, prints an error message indicating that the base and height must be positive numbers.
7. If the values are valid, calculates the area of the triangle using the formula:
   - Area = (base * height) / 2
8. Prints the calculated area.

Solution:

```python
# Ask for the base and height of the triangle
base = float(input("Enter the base of the triangle: "))
height = float(input("Enter the height of the triangle: "))

# Check if the base and height are positive
if base > 0 and height > 0:
    # Calculate the area
    area = (base * height) / 2
    print("Area of the triangle =", area)
else:
    # Print error message
    print("Error: Both the base and height must be positive numbers.")
```

Solution 35

Write a Python program that:
4. Asks the user to input an integer.
5. Determines if the number is even or odd using the modulus operator %.
6. Prints a message stating whether the number is even or odd.

Solution:

```python
# Ask the user to input a number
n = int(input("Enter an integer: "))

# Determine if the number is even or odd
if n % 2 == 0:
    print(n, "is an even number.")
else:
    print(n, "is an odd number.")
```

Solution 36

Write a Python program to find and print the greatest number in the `list = [10, 12, 23, 14, 3, 6]`.

Solution:

```python
# List of numbers
numbers = [10, 12, 23, 14, 3, 6]

# Initialize the maximum variable with the first element of the list
max_num = numbers[0]

# Iterate through the list to find the maximum number
for num in numbers:
    if num > max_num:
        max_num = num

# Print the greatest number
print("The greatest number is:", max_num)
```

Solution 37

Write a Python program that prints a list of the first 100 integers (from 1 to 100).

Solution:

```python
# Create an empty list to store integers
numbers = []

# Generate integers from 1 to 100
for i in range(1, 101):  # Start from 1, go up to 100 (inclusive)
    numbers.append(i)

# Print the list of integers
print(numbers)
```

Solution 38

Write a Python program that creates a list of tuples, where each tuple contains a key-value pair, like `t =` `[('a', 1), ('b', 2), ('c', 3)]`.
Then, convert this list of tuples into a dictionary and print the resulting dictionary.

Solution:

```python
# Create a list of tuples with key-value pairs
key_value_pairs = [('a', 1), ('b', 2), ('c', 3)]

# Convert the list of tuples into a dictionary
result_dict = dict(key_value_pairs)

# Print the resulting dictionary
print(result_dict)
```

Solution 39

Write a Python program to create a dictionary that stores the frequency of each character in the `string` = `'consideration'`. Print the resulting dictionary.

Solution:

```python
string = 'consideration'

# Create an empty dictionary to store character frequencies
char_frequency = {}

# Iterate over the unique characters in the string
for char in set(string):
    count = 0
    # Count occurrences of the current character
    for letter in string:
        if char == letter:
            count += 1
    char_frequency[char] = count

# Print the resulting dictionary
print(char_frequency)
```

Solution 40

Write a Python program that:

4. Prompts the user to input a number.
5. Checks if the number is divisible by 3, 5, or 7.
6. Prints the results in a single `print ()` statement, using string formatting to clearly indicate whether the number is divisible by each of these numbers.

Solution:

```python
# Prompt the user for input
n = int(input("Enter a number: "))

# Check divisibility for 3, 5, and 7
if n % 3 == 0:
    divisibleBy3 = "is divisible by 3"
else:
    divisibleBy3 = "is not divisible by 3"

if n % 5 == 0:
    divisibleBy5 = "is divisible by 5"
else:
    divisibleBy5 = "is not divisible by 5"

if n % 7 == 0:
    divisibleBy7 = "is divisible by 7"
else:
    divisibleBy7 = "is not divisible by 7"

# Print the results
print(f"The number {n}:\n{divisibleBy3}\n{divisibleBy5}\n{divisibleBy7}")
```

Solution 41

Write a Python program that removes all empty strings (`' '`) and None values from the `list =` `['house', '', 'cat', '', 'chair', None]`. Prints the resulting list.

Solution:

```python
# Original list
my_list = ['house', '', 'cat', '', 'chair', None]

# Filter out empty strings and None values
filtered_list = []

for item in my_list:
    if item is not None and item != '':
        filtered_list.append(item)

# Print the resulting list
print(filtered_list)
```

Solution 42

Write a Python program that:

4. Prompts the user to input a value from the `list = [1, 2, 3, 1, 2, 4, 3, 1, 5, 4, 6, 4, 3, 2, 1]`.
5. Counts how many times the entered value appears in the list.
6. Prints the result.

Solution:

```python
# List of values
my_list = [1, 2, 3, 1, 2, 4, 3, 1, 5, 4, 6, 4, 3, 2, 1]

# Prompt user for input
n = int(input("Choose a value from the list: "))

# Count occurrences of the entered value
counter = 0
for item in my_list:
    if item == n:
        counter += 1

# Print the result
print(f'\nThe value {n} appears {counter} times in the list.')
```

Solution 43

Write a Python program that prints the length of the `list` = `[1, 2, 3, 4, 5, 6]` without using the `len()` function.

Solution:

```python
# Define the list of elements
my_list = [1, 2, 3, 4, 5, 6]

# Initialize a counter variable to track the number of elements
counter = 0

# Loop through each element in the list and increment the counter for each element
for element in my_list:
    counter += 1

# Print the total number of elements in the list using string formatting
print('The list contains {} elements.'.format(counter))
```

Solution 44

Write a Python program that asks the user to input their name and then prints the message:
`"Hello, [username]"`.

Solution:

```python
# Ask the user to input their name
name = input('Enter your name: ')

# Print a greeting message with the user's name
# The `print()` function concatenates the greeting and the inputted name
print('Hello,', name)
```

Solution 45

Write a Python program that:
4. Asks the user to enter a string.
5. Prints each character of the string on a separate line.
6. Displays the total number of characters in the string.

Solution:

```python
# Ask the user to enter a string
string = input('Enter a word or phrase: ')

# Initialize a counter variable to count characters
count = 0

# Loop through each character in the string
for char in string:
    # Increment the counter by 1 for each character
    count += 1
    # Print the current character on a separate line
    print(char)

# Print the total number of characters in the string
print('Total number of characters:', count)
```

Solution 46

Write a Python program that finds and prints the index positions of every occurrence of the character 'i' in the `string = "I like this song"`.

Solution:

```python
# Define the string
s = "I like this song"

# Define the character to search for
char_to_find = 'n'

# Iterate through each index of the string
for i in range(len(s)):
    # Check if the character at the current index matches the target character
    if s[i] == char_to_find:
        # Print the index position if a match is found
        print('Index:', i)
```

Write a Python program that:
4. Defines the `string = "Who could I ever be, then as now, if not myself?"`.
5. Counts the number of vowels in the string, considering both uppercase and lowercase letters.
6. Prints the total number of vowels in the string.

Solution:

```python
# Define the string
s = "Who could I ever be, then as now, if not myself?"

# List of vowels to check (both lowercase and uppercase)
vowels = ['a', 'e', 'i', 'o', 'u', 'A', 'E', 'I', 'O', 'U']

# Initialize a counter for the vowels
vowel_count = 0

# Iterate through each character in the string
for char in s:
    # Check if the character is a vowel
    if char in vowels:
        # Increment the vowel counter
        vowel_count += 1

# Print the total number of vowels in the string
print('The string contains', vowel_count, 'vowels')
```

Solution 48

Write a Python program that adds a new key-value pair `6: 'f'` to the `dictionary = {1: 'a',
2: 'b', 3: 'c', 4: 'd', 5: 'e'}`. Print the updated dictionary.

Solution:

```python
# Define the initial dictionary with key-value pairs
d = {1: 'a', 2: 'b', 3: 'c', 4: 'd', 5: 'e'}

# Add a new key-value pair (6: 'f') to the dictionary
d[6] = 'f'

# Print the updated dictionary to show the new key-value pair
print(d)
```

Solution 49

Write a Python program that:

4. Defines a `dictionary = {'A': 1, 'B': 2, 'C': 3}`.
5. Checks if the key 'A' exists in the dictionary.
6. Prints a message indicating whether the key 'A' is present in the dictionary or not.

Solution:

```python
# Define the dictionary with key-value pairs
d = {'A': 1, 'B': 2, 'C': 3}

# Check if the key 'A' exists in the dictionary
if 'A' in d:
    print('Key found')
else:
    print('Key not found')
```

Solution 50

Write a Python program that:

3. Defines a `dictionary = {'a': 1, 'b': 2, 'c': 3}`.
4. Loops through the dictionary and prints each key-value pair in the format: key -> value.

Solution:

```python
# Define the dictionary with key-value pairs
d = {'a': 1, 'b': 2, 'c': 3}

# Loop through the dictionary and print each key-value pair in the format "key -> value"
for key, value in d.items():
    print(f'{key} -> {value}')
```

Author's note

For any suggestions or constructive criticism regarding the contents of this volume, please feel free to contact us at: CodeBooksProject@gmx.com

Python is a constantly evolving universe. With frequent updates and new versions, we're already on the third major release. New modules and features are regularly introduced to enhance the core package. If you need a resource on specific topics, feel free to suggest it, and I'll do my best to compile a dedicated book of exercises.

Acknowledgments

A sincere thank you to the reader who purchased this book. Your support, both through your purchase and financial contribution, will encourage the creation of future books. Thank you again!